© *Illustrations:* Colour Library International Ltd. 1977

©*Text:* David Gibbon C.L.I.

First published in Great Britain in 1975 by
Colour Library International Limited, England.

Designed and Produced by Ted Smart C.L.I.

Printed in Spain by CAYFOSA
bound by EUROBINDER-Barcelona

Filmsetting by Focus Photoset 90-94 Clerkenwell Road, London EC1.

Colour Library International Limited
80-82 Coombe Road, New Malden, Surrey, England
Telephone 01-942 7781
ISBN 0 904681 33 5

COOMBE BOOKS

LONDON

A PICTURE BOOK TO REMEMBER HER BY

The Collegiate Church of St. Peter in Westminster, *above*,
under its less formal title of Westminster Abbey, holds
within its walls a wealth of history. When entering the
Cathedral one cannot help pausing and gazing in awe at the
richness of this building. The view here is of the choir stalls
looking towards the highly-decorated organ loft and
stained-glass windows of the West Entrance.

Designed by Sir Christopher Wren and built between 1675 and 1710 of Portland Stone at a cost of £1,000,000 – a considerable sum at the time – St. Paul's, *below*, is the burial place of many famous men – Nelson, the Duke of Wellington and the painter, Turner to name but a few. In 1965 the State Funeral of Sir Winston Churchill was held here. The height of the building, including the cross, is 365 ft.

On the banks of the wonderful 'Old Father Thames', the Festival Hall, *above*, was originally built in 1951 for the Festival of Britain. It comprises several concert halls and smaller rooms for intimate recitals. It has been expanded as part of the South Bank Development which includes the National Film Theatre. The modern aspect of creamy white stone blends well with the traditional London.

The Post Office Tower, *right*, London's highest landmark–620 feet from ground level to masthead. With three observation platforms, from which superb views of London may be enjoyed, a cocktail lounge and a revolving restaurant, the Post Office Tower has quickly become popular with visitors to London.

Overleaf–Trafalgar Square.

London's year-round programme of ceremonies provides an unforgettable show of pageantry and tradition. The Beefeaters, *below*, fascinate all visitors to the Tower of London. One of the highlights of the year is undoubtedly the Trooping the Colour ceremony, *right*, which never fails to draw huge crowds of spectators. On the following six pages are further examples of the colour and precision of this part of the life of London.

Trafalgar Square *above*, is one of London's best known landmarks, laid out by Sir Charles Barry in 1829. From the top of the 182 ft. high column the statue of Nelson looks down on the Square, the fountains and its famous pigeons. Among the buildings which encircle Trafalgar Square are the National Gallery and St. Martin's-in-the-Fields, which is the parish church of Buckingham Palace.

Founded in 1753–a public lottery was set up to raise the money–the British Museum, *left*, is today an establishment of mammoth size. In it is stored a wealth of material of historic and artistic interest *plus* the National Library.

The company of Sotheby's, *below*, is the world's oldest and largest auctioneers of fine art pictures, wines, jewellery, silver, furniture, books, works of art, glass, musical instruments, and antiquities. Visitors can attend auctions and see a fabulous range of works, normally on view before the auction.

The Natural History Museum, *left*, houses a wealth of exhibits ranging from the huge displays to be seen in the Whale Gallery and, of course, the ever popular Dinosaurs, to a collection of a quarter of a million butterflies.

At Madame Tussaud's Waxwork Exhibition, *left*, in addition to its models of the famous and infamous are the London Planetarium, designed and equipped to educate the young, and a thunderous representation of the Battle of Trafalgar.

The Wellington Museum at Apsley House, *right*, is an establishment which must be visited. The House was once the home of the Duke of Wellington and contains, together with important collections of Spanish, Italian and Dutch paintings (by such masters as Valasquez, Murillo, Corregio, Pieter de Hooch and Jan Steen), many relics of the great Duke – medals, decorations, swords, flags, porcelain, silver plate and snuff boxes.

Outstandingly popular are the Science Museum, *far left*, with its vintage locomotives and aeroplanes and its wealth of working models, and the London Museum, *left*, which includes in its collection such fascinating items as flint implements, fire engines, toys from the 16th century and a model showing the Great Fire of London.

The following two pages show Piccadilly Circus, the night-time hub of the capital.

GUINNESS TIME

DOMINANT SITES LTD

AIR
INDIA

GOLD

One of the best

CINZAN[O]

THE BIANCO

SKOL

International

LAGER

LONDON'S LEADING JEWELLERS

LONGINES · FINE WATCHES · ROTARY

H. SAMUEL

CARTOONS
COMEDIES

H. SAMUEL · Saqui & Lawrence

PICCADILLY JEWELLERS

TLANTIC DAILY to NEW YORK

Bustling with crowds every moment of the day and every day of the year London's Regent Street, *above left*, and Oxford Street, *above and left*, can rightly be regarded as one of the finest shopping centres in the world. In its great department stores almost everything desired can be found.

Below, are four aspects of the stalls and people that make up the character of the Portobello Road. During the week the stalls display fruit and vegetables but on Saturdays they are crammed with mirrors, antiques, old gramophone records, chairs and silver.

From the top of the page: Harrods' Fish Hall, Burlington Arcade, Piccadilly and King's Road, Chelsea.

Overleaf, the Tower of London.

Westminster Abbey, *above*, where, since 1066, all but two of England's monarchs have been crowned and where many of them lie buried. In Poets' Corner memorials may be found to such famous bards as Chaucer, Shakespeare and Milton.

The Chapel of Henry VII, *right*, in Westminster Abbey dates from 1502 – a masterpiece of architectural grace and beauty. Hanging above the stalls of the Chapel and the tomb of Henry VII and his queen are the resplendent banners of the Knights of the Bath. The grounds of Kenwood House, *left*, are the picturesque setting for an open-air concert.

From the top of the page: Carols in the Tower of London, Downing Street–the official residence of the Prime Minister–and one of the many treasures to be seen in the Tower of London. *Overleaf.* The breathtaking view across the river from the south bank.

Everywhere in London the old and the new, the modern and the traditional, vie with each other. London is not just its buildings, its modern steel and glass, its Wren churches and cathedrals or its Law Courts. London is its people; the businessmen hurrying through the city, a 'clippie' talking to her driver, bewigged members of the legal profession in the Inns of Court, the Lord Mayor's coachman and resplendent 'Pearly' King and Queen.

While autumn in London is no longer a season of mists and mellow fruitfulness it still has very much its own atmosphere. The days grow shorter and, through the golden half-light, the horse-riders trot along famous Rotten Row, *left*. But, crowning London's year is winter– when the night falls early and the friendly lights of London glitter along every street and in every square. Pictured in Trafalgar Square, is the Christmas tree which Norway presents to the city every year.

London is by no means all crowded thoroughfares and historic buildings. There are peaceful parks in abundance all over the city and, once in them, it is hard to imagine that the bustling life of London is still going on all around. A city would indeed be a dreary place if it was not for these pleasant oases of green.

The setting sun, *overleaf,* shows up the delicate tracery of Tower Bridge and the surrounding cranes and paints the mighty Thames in shades of gold.

London's eating houses offer a wide variety of excellent food and, perhaps most important, can be fun to visit.

The street cries of London may have largely disappeared but reminders of the flower sellers who once sold their 'violets – lovely violets' at the foot of the statue of Eros in Picadilly Circus remain, and there is no shortage of flower stalls throughout London.

Markets are places for finding bargains. They are also, invariably, places of entertainment, and there arc both to be found, in plenty, in the many street markets selling a wide variety of merchandise to the accompaniment of typical banter.

Without its river, London would never have become the great city that it is today. There are many aspects of the river to be seen in London but the way that the city has grown up around it can be seen to greatest advantage in an aerial photograph, *above*, or from one of the many bridges that span its waters, *left*.

Down river from London is Greenwich, famous for its meridian, Royal Naval College and National Maritime Museum. Preserved permanently in dry dock at Greenwich lies the Cutty Sark, *right*, last and most famous of the old tea-clippers. Housed on board is a colourful and evocative collection of ship's figureheads which vividly recall the romantic days of sail.

St. Paul's Cathedral, Sir Christopher Wren's masterpiece, *above*.

Westminster Abbey looking towards the Houses of Parliament and Big Ben, *right*.
Houses of Parliament, *below*, from across the River.

Gazing resolutely across Parliament Square the statue, *above*, of one of England's most famous sons, Sir Winston Churchill.

Beefeaters, *below*, marching to take up their duties in the Tower of London.

Trooping the Colour, *below*, which takes place early in June, each year, in honour of the Queen's birthday, is London's most spectacular military pageant. This many-splendoured event is staged on the great parade ground behind Horse Guards. Her Majesty rides side-saddle from Buckingham Palace to Horse Guards at the head of the Household Cavalry. There she inspects the regimental colour which is trooped and reviews the Guards as they march and countermarch, to and fro across the parade ground.

The Lord Mayor's Show, *left*, a colourful procession believed to date from the 13th century. It occurs annually, in early November, when the newly-elected Lord Mayor—surrounded by pikemen and riding in a gilded coach—proceeds in State through the City.

That familiar London figure the Chelsea Pensioner, *above*, and the equally familiar Chelsea flower show are both to be found in the grounds of the Chelsea Hospital, founded by Charles II for old soldiers.

The Life Guards, *right*, riding down the Mall after their tour of duty.

Cheyne Walk, Chelsea, *left*, famous for its literary and artistic associations. It was here that George Eliot lived and died in 1880, a neighbour of Dante Gabriel Rossetti. And in Cheyne Row (a 'tributary' of the Walk) Thomas Carlyle and his wife had their London home.

The unfamiliar sight, *above*, of a deserted Fleet Street, normally a hive of activity, and the elegant dome of St. Paul's in the distance.

London is the background against which a host of famous fictional characters played their parts. None of these is better known than Sherlock Holmes whose many strange adventures put Baker Street and the gas-lit world around it on the map.

Two London policeman stand, unperturbed, *right*, amidst a whirl of London buses.

London caters to a wide variety of tastes. The visitor can find entertainment or interest at every turn. Theatres, cinemas and nightclubs abound; there are famous and historic places to visit, ceremonies to watch and, of course, some of the finest shops in the world.

The seasons transform a city.
In the spring a carpet of crocuses
and daffodils in the parks lend a
new delight to familiar sights.

High vantage points, *above*, afford fascinating glimpses of the changing face of the city.

The ever-increasing volume of air traffic using London's Heathrow airport, *left*, and the new generation of big jets, have meant constant enlargement and redesign of facilities. This is essential in order to be able to cope with machines such as the sleek new Concorde, *far left*.

The procession winds its way, *right*, from Windsor Castle, with the Royal Standard flying, at the ceremony of the Order of the Garter. The castle, *left*, from across the river and, *below*, from the air, first became a royal home during the reign of Henry I, although it was founded some years earlier by his father, William the Conqueror.

Overleaf. Contained within the walls of Windsor Castle is some of the finest architecture in England, as is evident from this magnificent view of St. George's Chapel.

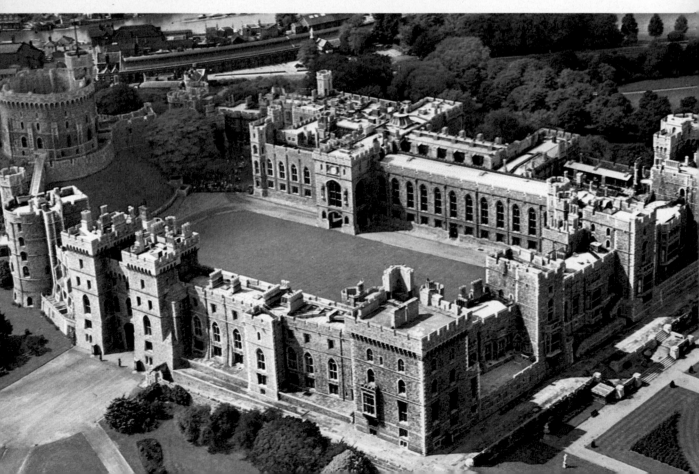